february quiet between frost and bloom

A Cozy Creative Prompt Journal with Creative Writing and Art Prompts for Late Winter into Early Spring

arden lane

contents

1. WELCOME — 1
2. HOW TO USE THIS BOOK — 4
3. FEBRUARY REFLECTIONS — 8
4. PROMPTS FOR FEBRUARY REFLECTIONS — 11
5. WINTER COMFORT CREATIVE PROMPTS — 19
6. PROMPTS FOR WINTER COMFORT — 22
7. THE LIMINAL SEASON — 31
8. PROMPTS FOR THE LIMENAL SEASON — 34
9. EARLY SPRING AWAKENING — 43
10. PROMPTS FOR EARLY SPRING AWAKENING — 46
11. THE FEBRUARY PROMPT PATH — 57
    A gentle 28 day journey from winter quiet toward early spring awakening. — 59
12. COZY CREATIVE RITUALS — 88
13. PROMPTS FOR COZY CREATIVE RITUALS — 91
    Morning Rituals — 92
    Midday Reset Rituals — 95
    Evening Wind Down Rituals — 98
14. CLOSING NOTES INTO SPRING — 101

welcome
. . .

Every year there is a small pocket of time when winter has begun to tire but spring has not quite found its voice. The world feels quieter than usual, almost paused, as if holding its breath. Light arrives a little earlier and lingers a little longer. Branches keep their bare shapes yet carry a hint of promise. Even the air feels different, softer, as though it is preparing for something it cannot rush. This in between moment is where our creative journey begins.

PEOPLE WHO SEARCH for winter to spring inspiration are often looking for a feeling rather than a destination. They want emotional grounding and a sense of seasonal identity. They want to understand why this time of year feels both heavy and hopeful at once. They want a way to capture that feeling and turn it into something personal. This chapter opens that doorway for you by guiding you from the deep quiet of winter toward the first glimmers of early spring.

Creativity in late winter can feel slow. Energy can dip. The world outside is pale and muted. Yet this slowness is not a barrier. It is an invitation. When everything around you moves gently, your inner world has more room to speak. This is why the soft transition is such a powerful time to create. It asks nothing loud or dramatic from you. Instead it encourages you to notice, reflect, and slowly warm up again.

Think of this chapter as a winter to spring creative guide that helps you reconnect with yourself. Here you will begin to sense the subtle change in your surroundings, the quiet lifting of your mood, and the tiny sparks of imagination returning. These are the qualities that make late winter inspiration so special. Renewal has not yet fully arrived, but the shape of it is beginning to form. You are not expected to rush. You are only asked to be present.

. . .

February Quiet Between Frost and Bloom

Let this chapter be your landing place. Settle into the gentle hush of the season and let your thoughts stretch like the lengthening daylight. You have stepped into the soft transition. From here, every prompt and page will carry you a little farther into the warmth ahead.

how to use this book
. . .

CREATIVITY DOES NOT LOOK the same for everyone, and it does not behave the same every day for the same person either. Some days you feel full of ideas. Other days you feel quiet, tired or unsure. This journal is built to meet you in all of those states, not just on your best days. You are welcome here exactly as you are.

You can use this book daily, a few times a week or only when a small spark appears and you feel ready to catch it.

There is no single right way. Some readers like to start at the beginning and move through the pages in order, treating it like a gentle course. Others prefer to open the journal at random and trust whatever prompt arrives that day. Both approaches are perfectly valid. Think of this book as a companion, not a teacher with rules.

This is a creative prompt journal for adults, which means the prompts are written with emotional depth and quiet honesty in mind. They invite you to notice what is happening in your inner world and in the season around you. You will find a mix of writing prompts, sketch prompts and small mindfulness moments. On some pages, you will be asked to describe, remember, imagine or reflect in words. On others, you will be invited to draw, doodle or map out feelings visually.

February Quiet Between Frost and Bloom

On certain days you might feel like filling the page with flowing paragraphs. On other days you might only manage a few words and a quick sketch in the corner. Both are enough. What matters most is not how much you produce, but that you show up with a little curiosity and a willingness to listen to yourself. Even a ten second response can shift how you feel inside your day.

If you are someone who enjoys structure, you may find comfort in the February Prompt Path. This section gathers daily creativity prompts into a 28 day journey that follows the natural rhythm of the month. It begins in the deeper quiet of late winter and gradually moves toward early spring energy. You can treat it like a soft creative routine. Open to the day's prompt, respond in whatever way feels possible, then close the book knowing you have gently tended to your imagination.

If you prefer a looser flow, feel free to wander. Let your eye fall on any prompt that calls to you. Perhaps you will be drawn to the winter comfort pages on a day when you feel tired. Another day you might feel pulled toward early spring awakening or liminal season prompts. You might even use the journal seasonally rather than daily, dipping in whenever late winter returns and you want to reconnect with this particular mood.

You can also layer your use of the book. For example

Choose one writing prompt for the week and return to it several times, adding new thoughts as they arise.

Pair a sketch prompt from one section with a reflection from another.

Use a page in the evening to unwind and another in the morning to set a gentle tone for the day.

Make it your own.

There is no quiz at the end and no expectation that every page will be used or finished. Some prompts may not resonate right now. You can skip them. You might come back to them another year when the season of your life has changed.

If you enjoy journaling, you can treat this book as a companion to your regular notebook.

You might answer a prompt here, then continue the thought in your usual journal. If you are new to creative practice, let this book be a low pressure doorway. The prompts are deliberately simple and spacious so that you do not feel overwhelmed.

You can also use this journal alongside other cozy practices. Light a candle. Make a warm drink. Wrap yourself in a blanket. Let the setting support you. Even five minutes of quiet attention with one prompt can offer a sense of grounding that lasts long after you close the book.

Most of all, let the season guide the pace.

Late winter has its own tempo. It moves slowly and gently. You are not required to race through the pages or achieve anything grand. Creativity in this time of year is more like breathing out than climbing up. It softens, releases, and makes room.

Some days you will meet a prompt and feel ready to dive deep. Other days you will glance at one line, write a single sentence, and that will be enough.

Trust that this is still valuable. Trust that small steps count.

Take your time. Pause when you need to. Skip, revisit, circle and wander. This book is here to hold space for you as you move from the quiet of winter toward the first hints of bloom. Creativity does not rush through late winter. It settles in, listens carefully and slowly begins to thaw.

february reflections
...

FEBRUARY CARRIES a mood unlike any other month. It settles over the days like a light blanket, soft but steady, and it encourages you to pause in ways other months do not. The world feels muted and introspective, as if everything has stepped one pace back to catch its breath. Yet even within all that quiet, hints of change appear at the edges. A slightly brighter morning. A shift in the way air moves. A small bud that was not there the day before. This chapter invites you into that tender space where stillness and subtle awakening live side by side.

These pages are meant to help you ease into the emotional landscape of February. Here you will find gentle check ins and slow reflections that encourage honesty without pressure. You will be guided to notice things you might usually overlook. How your energy rises or dips throughout the day. How the light behaves in your home. Which emotions tend to echo inside you during late winter. These small observations become stepping stones to deeper awareness. They help you understand yourself with kindness rather than judgment.

> *People who search for cozy or mindful seasonal writing are often looking for a place where they can breathe. A place where their thoughts do not need to rush or perform. This space is created for that purpose.*

The prompts in this section are simple, open and calming. They ask you to pay attention in a soft way. To listen to your inner weather. To explore what feels heavy or what feels hopeful. To slow down long enough to hear the quiet wisdom of your own mind.

The February creativity prompts in this chapter are not tasks to complete. They are invitations to rest, reflect and reconnect. You can write as much or as little as you wish. You can return to the same prompt several times if it continues to speak to you. Some reflections may open doors you did not expect. Others may simply help you feel grounded for a moment. Both outcomes matter. Mindful seasonal writing tends to reveal its gifts slowly, and this month encourages exactly that pace. February asks you to soften. To be patient. To take things one small step at a time.

This chapter also forms the heart of the cozy creative journal tone. Every prompt is shaped to feel gentle and comforting. When you sit with these reflections, imagine yourself wrapped in a warm texture or surrounded by soft light. Allow yourself to be present without trying to push forward too quickly. This tenderness is not a weakness. It is fertile ground. It prepares you for the creative journey ahead by helping you settle into your own rhythm, rather than the rhythm of the outside world.

· · ·

Arden Lane

As you move through February Reflections, think of this chapter as a quiet room where you can place your thoughts down gently and explore them without hurry.

Notice what stirs when everything around you slows. Notice what brightens when you hold still long enough for clarity to arrive. This is your moment to breathe, observe and reconnect with yourself before the season begins to shift into something new.

Let these reflections be your anchor. Let them steady you. February has its own soft wisdom, and you are stepping right into it.

prompts for
february reflections

. . .

A SOFT AND INTROSPECTIVE BEGINNING.

Arden Lane

1 Describe the quietest moment of your day and what it reveals about you.

2 Write about a color that feels like February and why.

3 Sketch something small that brought you comfort this week.

February Quiet Between Frost and Bloom

4 Describe a feeling that visits you often in late winter.

5 Write how your morning light changes through the month.

6 Draw a tiny symbol that represents your current emotional state.

Arden Lane

7 Reflect on a gentle truth you learned this season.

8 Write about the last time you felt deeply rested.

9 Sketch an object that feels safe to you and write why.

10 Describe a moment of stillness that surprised you.

11 Write three things you notice about the world when you move slowly.

12 Sketch the outline of a cozy corner and fill it with textures.

Arden Lane

13 Write about a memory connected to cold air or frost.

14 Reflect on the sound of winter and describe its tone.

15 Draw a simple pattern that feels like calm.

February Quiet Between Frost and Bloom

16 Write about the space between what you need and what you want.

17 Describe a small pleasure that February brings you.

18 Sketch one thing you would like to protect or hold close.

19 Write about a feeling that softened recently.

20 Reflect on what February has taught you about yourself.

winter comfort
creative prompts
. . .

WINTER SPEAKS in a language that is softer than words. You can hear it in the muffled quiet of snow when the world seems wrapped in cotton. You can feel it in the weight of blankets that settle over you like a gentle reassurance. You see it in the warm glow of a lamp in the corner of a dark room, casting calm shapes on the walls. Winter often feels like a season that tucks you away, not to hide you, but to give you space to breathe and gather yourself. This chapter invites you to explore that comforting atmosphere and turn it into creative expression.

The prompts here are shaped for readers who long for rest and warmth during the colder months. Many people come to winter seeking stillness, introspection or a sense of refuge, and these pages help you lean into that mood. You will find yourself describing your ideal winter nook, the texture of a cherished blanket or a memory softened by snow. Some prompts will draw you into writing, encouraging you to explore the stories, sensations and emotions that winter stirs. Others will guide you into sketching the small visual details that make this season feel gentle and safe.

This blend of writing and drawing is deliberate. Creativity in late winter often becomes deeper when you engage more than one sense.

Your mind sinks into the quiet more fully when your hands are moving. Lines and shapes can express comfort in ways words sometimes cannot, and words can capture meaning that images only hint at. When both come together, they create a warm inner landscape that feels rich and soothing.

This chapter also supports the purpose of this journal as a bridge between winter and early spring. The creative writing prompts winter spring theme is woven into these pages by grounding you in the safe stillness of winter while subtly preparing you for the season that follows. Winter comfort has a way of nourishing creativity from the inside out, allowing you to rest so that new ideas can form in their own time.

The visual exercises offered here turn the book into a seasonal art prompts journal as well. You may find yourself sketching the soft halo of candlelight, the delicate pattern of frost on a window or the cozy folds of knitted fabric. These exercises encourage your attention to slow down and linger, which is exactly what winter invites us to practice. The pace is calm. The tone is quiet. The experience is meant to feel like sitting under a blanket on a cold day, content and protected.

Treat this chapter like a warm drink. Let it soothe you. Let it remind you that creativity does not always need to be bold or expansive. Sometimes it thrives in small, comforting spaces. Sometimes the gentlest moments carry the deepest inspiration. Allow winter's soft language to guide you. Let the prompts lead you inward, where warmth gathers and imagination begins to glow again.

February Quiet Between Frost and Bloom

prompts for winter comfort
. . .

WARMTH, softness and gentle introspection.

21 Describe your perfect winter evening.

22 Sketch a winter comfort object and imagine its secret history.

23 Write about a scent that reminds you of warmth.

Arden Lane

. . .

24 Draw a cup of tea or coffee and write the memory it brings up.

25 Describe the feeling of stepping inside after cold weather.

February Quiet Between Frost and Bloom

26 Write a scene that takes place under a blanket.

27 Sketch the glow of candlelight using soft shading.

Arden Lane

28 Write about a winter habit that soothes you.

29 Draw the shape of warmth as you imagine it.

30 Describe a winter sound that comforts you.

February Quiet Between Frost and Bloom

31 Write about a moment you felt sheltered.

32 Sketch an abstract pattern inspired by snowflakes.

33 Write about something you cherish more in winter than any other season.

34 Draw a winter window view from your imagination.

35 Describe the feeling of slow mornings.

February Quiet Between Frost and Bloom

36 Write a letter to yourself on a cold day.

37 Sketch a soft fabric texture that calms you.

38 Describe a winter ritual you secretly enjoy.

Arden Lane

39 Write about a quiet conversation that stayed with you.

40 Sketch a symbol of warmth and let the lines feel gentle.

the liminal season

. . .

There is a delicate beauty in the space between what has been and what is becoming.

THIS CHAPTER IS DEVOTED to that quiet threshold where winter begins to soften and spring waits just out of sight. It is a space that feels both familiar and new, as if the world is holding its breath and preparing to turn the page. The edges of winter begin to blur. Snow feels lighter. Light stretches farther across the morning. Branches still look bare, yet you can sense the life gathering inside them. This liminal season is gentle, complex and full of emotion.

This is a time shaped by contrasts. Cold air brushes your skin while warm sunlight touches your face. The ground is still hard, but small buds begin to swell with promise. The days are slow and sleepy, yet hints of hope rise quietly beneath the surface. Every small shift feels meaningful because it arrives softly, without asking for attention. This chapter invites you to explore that subtle magic and turn it into creative expression.

Readers who are drawn to transitions often feel the emotional richness of this in between world. It is a place where two truths can exist at once. You can feel tired and hopeful. You can feel still and restless. You can feel ready and hesitant. The prompts in this section help you express these layered feelings through gentle themes of waiting, stirring, softness and renewal. They invite you to move slowly, to notice what is waking inside you and to honor the parts of yourself that are still resting.

Some prompts ask you to write scenes that balance two opposing moods, such as warmth meeting cold or darkness meeting growing light. Others guide you to sketch images that capture both stillness and motion, like a branch holding frost and buds at the same time. These small acts of creativity help you practice looking closely at the world and at yourself. They encourage you to see the complexity of this season rather than rushing past it.

This section reflects the heart of a late winter inspiration book. The liminal space is quiet, gentle and easy to overlook, yet it holds meaning you only discover when you slow down. These prompts help you explore that meaning in a personal way. They also support the role of this journal as a winter to spring creative guide by helping you tune into shifts that happen gradually, almost secretly. The more attention you give them, the more you notice how change unfolds in real life, not in grand leaps but in soft steps.

> *Let these prompts teach you how to hold two feelings at once without forcing one to overpower the other.*

This is the art of the liminal season. It is the art of being in between. It is the art of recognizing that transformation rarely arrives all at once. Instead, it whispers its way in, touches your edges, and slowly encourages you to open. Embrace this quiet, tender transition. There is beauty in the waiting and wisdom in the pause.

February Quiet Between Frost and Bloom

prompts for the
limenal season
. . .

THE IN BETWEEN world of late winter.

February Quiet Between Frost and Bloom

41 Write about the first moment you sensed winter beginning to fade.

42 Sketch a branch half frosted and half budding.

43 Describe a situation where you felt caught between two emotions.

44 Write a scene that holds both cold and warm tones.

45 Sketch a horizon that feels like possibility.

46 Write about waiting and what it has taught you.

47 Draw a shadow that looks ready to move.

48 Describe a day that felt both quiet and alive.

49 Write about a personal shift that began quietly.

50 Sketch two shapes that represent opposing moods.

February Quiet Between Frost and Bloom

51 Write a letter from your winter self to your spring self.

52 Draw something that is changing slowly.

53 Describe a space that feels suspended in time.

Arden Lane

54 Write about transition as if it were a character.

55 Sketch a doorway that leads toward something unknown.

56 Describe what you hope this soft season will reveal.

57 Write about a moment when you sensed the world stirring.

58 Draw an object with half in shadow, half in light.

Arden Lane

59 Describe the feeling of being almost ready.

60 Write about a quiet longing that grows in late winter.

early spring awakening
...

WHEN EARLY SPRING ARRIVES, it does not come with a shout. It slips in softly, the way a whisper drifts across a quiet room. You notice it first in small ways. A little more light resting on the windowsill. A bird call that sounds out of place during a still cold morning. A tiny sprout pushing through soil with a courage that seems far larger than its size. Early spring is gentle in its arrival. It does not try to impress. Instead, it invites you to notice the world waking up one delicate moment at a time.

This chapter helps you tune in to those early signs of life and use them as creative fuel. It is easy to overlook small beginnings when you are waiting for dramatic change, but early spring reminds you that true renewal often starts quietly. This is a season that teaches patience, curiosity and appreciation for subtle details. The prompts in this section guide you to slow down and pay attention to the way color returns piece by piece, how shadows shift as the sun climbs a little higher, and how the landscape begins to breathe again.

Many readers who seek seasonal inspiration want hope and brightness. They want to reconnect with the parts of themselves that feel fresh and alive. These prompts are designed to help you bring those qualities to the surface. You will write about emerging color, new beginnings and quiet forms of growth. You may find yourself sketching the first blossoms, the curve of a new leaf or the faint warmth of early sunshine. These small creative acts encourage you to open gently, just as the season does.

This chapter aligns with the purpose of seasonal art prompts by offering visual exercises that reflect this tender period of awakening. You are not asked to create bold or elaborate work. Instead, you are encouraged to sketch simple shapes, soft lines and pale tones that mirror the season itself. The pairing of writing and art deepens your connection to early spring because it invites multiple senses into the experience. What you draw supports what you write. What you write brings meaning to what you draw.

The tone of these pages also mirrors the quiet mood that still lingers from winter, creating a smooth and uplifting transition. Creativity does not need to leap from cold to bloom in one step. It can unfold gradually, warmed by sunlight and guided by the slow turning of the season. The prompts here help your imagination move toward possibility and forward momentum without losing the peaceful atmosphere of February. They place you in a space where you can feel both the remnants of winter and the beginnings of spring, which is where the richest inspiration often lives.

Think of this chapter as a slow opening. A gentle stretch after a long rest. A reminder that growth often starts with something small. Let these prompts bloom at their own pace. There is no need to hurry. Early spring knows how to unfold without force, and your creativity will follow the same rhythm when you give it room to breathe.

February Quiet Between Frost and Bloom

prompts for early spring awakening
. . .

A TENDER BEGINNING, where color returns one breath at a time.

February Quiet Between Frost and Bloom

61 Describe the earliest sign that the season is turning, even if it is barely there.

62 Sketch a small sprout or seedling and imagine what it wishes for.

63 Write about a moment when the air felt different, as though carrying a new mood.

64 Draw a gentle curve or line that captures the feeling of opening.

65 Describe a color returning to the world and how it changes your inner landscape.

66 Write about a part of your creativity that feels ready to wake from rest.

67 Sketch the silhouette of a blossom before it fully forms.

68 Describe a sound that reminds you the world is stirring again.

69 Write about a quiet beginning you almost overlooked.

70 Sketch a soft pattern inspired by new growth or tender leaves.

71 Describe the sensation of standing between the cold you know and the warmth you can sense coming.

72 Write about a hope that feels small but persistent, like a bud pressing through frost.

73 Sketch one early bloom using the faintest lines you can manage.

74 Describe how the light shifts in early spring and what that shift awakens in you.

75 Write a scene where something opens slowly and gently, as if testing the air.

76 Sketch a horizon touched by the first hint of color returning.

77 Describe a moment when your energy lifted unexpectedly, like sunlight breaking through cloud.

78 Write about what early spring teaches you about patience and trust.

79 Sketch a symbol that captures the courage of beginning again after stillness.

Arden Lane

80 Describe the softest change you noticed this week and what it meant to you.

81 Write about a dream or intention beginning to stretch after a long rest.

82 Sketch a budding branch and let each line feel like a breath.

83 Describe the way early spring invites you to move differently, speak differently or feel differently.

84 Write about something inside you that feels fragile yet hopeful, like early petals.

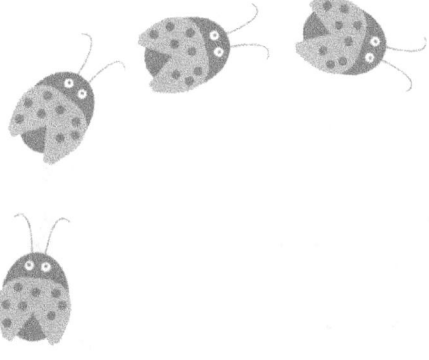

Arden Lane

85 Sketch a gentle doorway into possibility.

the february prompt path
...

SOME READERS FEEL MOST SUPPORTED when they have a clear and steady plan to follow. The February Prompt Path was created with that in mind. It offers a simple, structured journey through the entire month, guiding you one day at a time with prompts that blend writing, sketching and gentle reflection. This path gives shape to your creativity in a way that feels manageable and comforting, especially during a season when energy can be unpredictable.

The flow of these twenty eight days mirrors the season itself.

The early days of the month settle you into the quiet rhythm of winter. The prompts here draw your attention inward and help you rest, reflect and reconnect with your inner landscape. As the month progresses, the prompts begin to shift. You move into the soft transitional space where winter loosens its grip and something new begins to stir. These middle days guide you to explore the delicate balance of holding stillness and anticipation at the same time.

Toward the end of February, the prompts gently invite you toward early spring energy. They focus on hints of color, returning light and the first signs of renewal. The goal is not to rush you forward, but to help you open naturally to the season. This slow and intentional progression allows your creativity to shift alongside the world around you. The more you follow the rhythm, the more you begin to feel how creativity and season can move together.

> *Each daily prompt is brief enough to complete in just a few minutes, so it fits easily into your routine.*

Yet each one is rich enough to lead you deeper when you have the time or desire. You might write for two lines one day and fill a whole page the next. You might draw a simple symbol one morning and create something detailed the following afternoon. The February Prompt Path adapts to your energy rather than demanding consistency you cannot always give.

As a creative prompt journal for adults, this chapter provides a gentle structure that helps you build habits without pressure. When you show up to a prompt every day, even for a short moment, creativity becomes a natural part of your day instead of a task you must force. Over time, this rhythm creates a sense of steadiness, something especially meaningful during late winter when many people crave grounding.

These daily prompts also align with February creativity prompts by shaping the month into a clear path you can walk step by step. Each day offers a new moment of awareness, a small spark of imagination or a fresh way of seeing the season. Even if you use this section casually rather than daily, it still serves as a reliable source of direction whenever you need it.

You can follow the February Prompt Path from start to finish, or you can dip into it whenever you want inspiration or guidance. Both choices will lead you forward. This chapter is here to support you, not confine you. Think of it as a quiet companion for the month, walking beside you as winter softens and spring begins to whisper its arrival.

February Quiet Between Frost and Bloom

a gentle 28 day journey from winter quiet toward early spring awakening.

Begin here if you want a daily creative rhythm. Each prompt blends writing, sketching or reflection and can be completed in just a few minutes. Move through these pages at your own pace. Let the season guide you.

Arden Lane

Day 1

Write about the feeling of stepping into a new month that still carries winter's hush.

_____
_____
_____
_____
_____
_____
_____

Sketch a simple symbol that represents calm.

Day 2

Describe a winter memory that brings you comfort.

_____
_____
_____
_____
_____

Add a quick drawing of one object from that memory.

Arden Lane

Day 3

Notice the light at your window today. Write how it makes you feel.

_____
_____
_____
_____
_____
_____
_____
_____

Shade a small square showing its color.

Day 4

Write a short scene that takes place indoors during a cold evening.

_____
_____
_____
_____
_____
_____
_____
_____
_____
_____

Sketch one warm detail from the room.

Arden Lane

Day 5

Sit quietly for one minute. Write the first three words that come to mind.

_____

_____

_____

Turn one of those words into a tiny illustration.

Day 6

Imagine winter speaking to you. What would it say.

_____

_____

_____

Draw a small motif that matches its message.

Arden Lane

Day 7

Reflect on what you are carrying emotionally this season.

_____
_____
_____
_____
_____
_____
_____
_____

Sketch a container that could hold those feelings.

Day 8

Write about something that feels almost ready to change.

_____
_____
_____
_____
_____
_____
_____
_____
_____

Sketch a branch with one bud beginning to form.

Day 9

Describe a moment that holds both heaviness and hope.

_____
_____
_____
_____
_____
_____
_____
_____
_____

Use lines or color to represent each feeling.

February Quiet Between Frost and Bloom

Day 10

Write a short imagined dialogue between winter and spring.

_____
_____
_____
_____
_____
_____
_____
_____
_____
_____

Sketch a soft transition between two colors to show their meeting.

Arden Lane

Day 11

Think of a place you love when the world is quiet. Describe it slowly.

_____
_____
_____
_____
_____
_____
_____
_____
_____

Add a small drawing of one detail from that place.

February Quiet Between Frost and Bloom

Day 12

Write about waiting. What does waiting feel like in your body and mind.

_____
_____
_____
_____
_____
_____
_____
_____
_____
_____

Draw a shape that expresses stillness.

Arden Lane

Day 13

Describe something you noticed today that you often overlook.

_____
_____
_____
_____
_____
_____
_____
_____
_____

Sketch it as simply as possible.

February Quiet Between Frost and Bloom

Day 14

Write a gentle letter to yourself. Offer softness and patience.

_____
_____
_____
_____
_____
_____
_____
_____
_____

Decorate the page with one small motif that feels kind.

Arden Lane

Day 15

Write about the first sign of spring you remember noticing in past years.

_____
_____
_____
_____
_____
_____
_____
_____

Sketch the memory as a loose silhouette or outline.

February Quiet Between Frost and Bloom

Day 16

Describe a color that feels like renewal.

_____
_____
_____
_____
_____
_____
_____
_____
_____
_____

Fill a small space with that color.

Arden Lane

Day 17

Write a scene where something small begins.

_____
_____
_____
_____
_____
_____
_____
_____
_____

Draw a tiny sprout, seed or spark.

Day 18

Think of a dream or hope that has been sleeping. Write what might help it wake.

_____
_____
_____
_____
_____
_____
_____
_____
_____

Sketch a symbol of awakening.

Arden Lane

Day 19

Write about the feeling of fresh air on a slightly warmer day.

Draw the movement of that air with lines or curves.

February Quiet Between Frost and Bloom

Day 20

Describe a place that holds your imagination.

_____
_____
_____
_____
_____
_____
_____
_____
_____
_____

Sketch its doorway, window or threshold.

Arden Lane

Day 21

Write about a moment you felt light returning to your life.

_____
_____
_____
_____
_____
_____
_____
_____
_____

Add a small glow or halo of color on the page.

Day 22

Write about a part of yourself that feels ready to stretch or grow.

_____
_____
_____
_____
_____
_____
_____
_____
_____

Sketch the shape of that growth.

Arden Lane

Day 23

Describe a new habit or intention you want to plant this season.

_____
_____
_____
_____
_____
_____
_____
_____

Draw the soil or container it will grow from.

Day 24

Write about compassion for your winter self.

_____
_____
_____
_____
_____
_____
_____
_____
_____
_____

Illustrate it with soft, rounded lines.

Arden Lane

Day 25

Imagine early spring speaking to you. What gentle encouragement would it offer.

_____
_____
_____
_____
_____
_____
_____
_____
_____

Sketch a small early bloom to accompany its voice.

February Quiet Between Frost and Bloom

Day 26

Write about something you are releasing as winter fades.

Draw an open hand or an object drifting away.

Arden Lane

Day 27

Describe what creativity feels like for you right now.

_____
_____
_____
_____
_____
_____
_____
_____

Sketch a personal symbol of creative energy.

February Quiet Between Frost and Bloom

Day 28

Write a reflection on the month. What shifted. What softened. What grew.

_____
_____
_____
_____
_____
_____
_____
_____
_____
_____

Sketch either frost or bloom, depending on which feels true to your journey.

cozy creative rituals

. . .

CREATIVITY OFTEN GROWS IN SMALL, steady rituals rather than dramatic bursts of inspiration. These gentle practices help you build a rhythm that feels comforting and sustainable, especially during the long stretch of late winter when energy can feel low and the world outside moves slowly.

February Quiet Between Frost and Bloom

This chapter introduces simple rituals designed to support your mood, warm your imagination and give you small moments of connection throughout the day. Here you will find morning warmups that ease you into wakefulness, sensory check ins that anchor you in the present moment, mini sketch exercises that encourage play without pressure and short reflective pauses that help you notice what is shifting inside you. Each ritual is meant to be simple, soothing and easy to fold into daily life. You do not need long stretches of time or perfect focus. A few minutes of gentle attention is enough.

> *Readers who seek cozy creativity are often craving comfort rather than challenge.*

They want guidance that feels kind, rhythms that feel manageable and activities that make space for calm. The rituals in this chapter give you exactly that. They are small yet meaningful acts that encourage you to breathe a little deeper, soften your shoulders and reconnect with yourself in a quiet way. They remind you that creativity does not need to be loud or ambitious to be fulfilling. It can be soft, slow and nurturing.

These rituals also strengthen the identity of this book as a cozy creative journal. They add warmth to the experience of using the prompts and help you cultivate a sense of emotional safety around your creative practice. Think of them as gentle companions to the rest of the journal, supporting your process rather than directing it.

> *At the same time, these practices support mindful seasonal writing by deepening your awareness of the world around you.*

When you pause to notice the temperature of the air, the color of the sky or the sound of your environment, you become more attuned to the subtle shifts of the season.

When used regularly, these rituals keep your creative energy warm even on the coldest days. They help you stay connected to the soft light of February and the quiet potential of early spring.

Let these small acts steady you. Let them brighten your mornings, soften your evenings and gently support you as you move through the final weeks of winter. Creativity thrives when it is cared for. These rituals offer that care in the simplest, most comforting way.

Arden Lane

prompts for cozy creative rituals
. . .

Arden Lane

morning rituals

Gentle ways to wake creativity with warmth and ease.

1 SIT QUIETLY for one minute and notice the first sound you hear. Write a single line about how it shapes your morning.

_____

2 Sketch the shape of the light in your room right now.

3 Place your hand on your chest. Describe the feeling of your breath and how it moves.

_____
_____
_____

4 Write a soft intention for the day - only a few words.

_____

5 Sketch a small symbol that represents morning calm.

6 Open a window or imagine open air. Describe how the day feels before it truly begins.

_____
_____
_____

7 Notice your posture. Adjust gently. Write how the small shift affects your mood.

_____
_____
_____

Arden Lane

8 Sketch something within arm's reach without overthinking the lines.

9 Write one thing your creativity needs from you today.

10 Sketch a gentle pattern inspired by your first sip of tea or coffee.

midday reset rituals

Simple pauses that help you reconnect with presence during slow or busy afternoons.

11 Step away from what you are doing and look at the nearest window. Write the first three details you notice outside.

_____
_____
_____

12 Sketch a tiny moment of movement, such as a leaf shifting or light crossing the floor.

13 Place both feet on the ground. Describe how the support feels.

_____
_____
_____

14 Write a sentence about the temperature of the air and how it touches your skin.

_____

15 Sketch a soft curve that represents release.

16 Close your eyes for ten seconds. Write the first color that comes to mind.

_____

17 Sketch a corner of the room using only simple outlines.

18 Write a note of kindness to your afternoon self.

_____
_____
_____

February Quiet Between Frost and Bloom

19 Sketch a tiny object that often goes unnoticed during your day.

20 Write about one thing you can let go of before evening arrives.

_____

evening wind down rituals

Slow, calming practices to help creativity rest and settle.

21 Dim the lights or imagine dimness. Write one thing that softened inside you today.

_____

22 Sketch a shape that feels like quiet.

[ ]

23 Notice the heaviest part of your body and describe the sensation.

_____
_____
_____

24 Write a gentle reflection on something that surprised you, even if it was small.

_____
_____
_____

25 Sketch a calming texture, such as soft loops or flowing lines.

26 Hold something warm, like a mug or blanket. Write about the comfort it gives.

27 Sketch a symbol that represents closure for the day.

28 Write a sentence about your evening mood as if it were weather.

29 Sketch your hand in a relaxed position with loose, unfussy lines.

30 Write one thing you want to carry with you into tomorrow.

_____

closing notes into spring

. . .

AS WINTER FADES completely and spring begins to rise, your creativity naturally shifts with the season. The quiet weight of February lifts, and a new and gentle brightness begins to take its place. This chapter is your invitation to pause and reflect on what this month has offered you. You are encouraged to think about how your thoughts, emotions and creative energy have changed, even in small ways. Transitioning from February into March is not a sudden leap. It is a soft turning point, and you deserve a moment to honor it.

Throughout this journal, you have been moving slowly from winter stillness toward early spring awakening. This final chapter allows you to look back on that journey with warmth and curiosity. What did this month help you notice. What softened inside you. What new ideas began to form. What parts of yourself felt ready to rest, and what parts felt ready to grow. These reflections help you see how creativity responds to the seasons just as the natural world does.

People who are drawn to seasonal creativity often seek ongoing connection rather than a single month of prompts. The closing notes in this chapter are written with that desire in mind. They encourage you to continue writing, drawing and observing as spring unfolds around you. You are guided to consider what you want to nurture in the coming weeks and what you may choose to release as winter fully slips away. You can reflect on what early spring inspiration feels like within you and how you might welcome more of that feeling into your days.

This chapter completes your winter to spring creative guide, but it does not close your creative path. It simply opens it in a new direction.

Creativity does not end when February ends. It changes shape. It follows the season into fresh air, brighter light and unfolding growth. You may find that some prompts from earlier chapters speak to you differently now. You may return to your favorites with new insight. You may even create your own rituals or prompts inspired by what you discovered here.

Let these closing reflections remind you that growth is a gentle process.

You do not need to have everything figured out by the first day of March. You only need to continue moving with intention and softness. As spring rises, so will your creativity, one quiet moment at a time.

February Quiet Between Frost and Bloom

www.ingramcontent.com/pod-product-compliance
Lightning Source LLC
Chambersburg PA
CBHW051419070526
44584CB00023B/3496